WHY AMERICAN ELECTIONS ARE FLAWED (AND HOW TO FIX THEM)

McCourtney Institute for Democracy

The Pennsylvania State University's McCourtney Institute for Democracy (http://democracyinstitute.la.psu.edu) was founded in 2012 as an interdisciplinary center for research, teaching, and outreach on democracy. The institute coordinates innovative programs and projects in collaboration with the Center for American Political Responsiveness and the Center for Democratic Deliberation.

Laurence and Lynne Brown Democracy Medal

The Laurence and Lynne Brown Democracy Medal recognizes outstanding individuals, groups, and organizations that produce exceptional innovations to further democracy in the United States or around the world. In even numbered years, the medal spotlights practical innovations, such as new institutions, laws, technologies, or movements that advance the cause of democracy. Awards given in odd numbered years highlight advances in democratic theory that enrich philosophical conceptions of democracy or empirical models of democratic behavior, institutions, or systems.

WHY AMERICAN ELECTIONS ARE FLAWED (AND HOW TO FIX THEM)

PIPPA NORRIS

CORNELL SELECTS

An imprint of

CORNELL UNIVERSITY PRESS

Ithaca and London

Cornell Selects, *an imprint of Cornell University Press, provides a forum for advancing provocative ideas and fresh viewpoints through outstanding digital and print publications. Longer than an article and shorter than a book, titles published under this imprint explore a diverse range of topics in a clear and concise format—one designed to appeal to any reader. Cornell Selects publications continue the Press's long tradition of supporting high quality scholarship and sharing it with the wider community, promoting a culture of broad inquiry that is a vital aspect of the mission of Cornell University.*

First published 2016 by Cornell University Press

Printed in the United States of America

Library of Congress Cataloging-in-Publication Data

Names: Norris, Pippa, author.
Title: Why American elections are flawed (and how to fix them) / Pippa Norris.
Description: Ithaca : Cornell Selects, an imprint of Cornell University Press, 2017. | Includes bibliographical references.
Identifiers: LCCN 2016049427 (print) | LCCN 2016058054 (ebook) | ISBN 9781501713408 (pbk. : alk. paper) | ISBN 9781501713415 (epub/mobi) | ISBN 9781501713774 (pdf)
Subjects: LCSH: Elections—United States—Management. | Elections—Corrupt practices—United States.
Classification: LCC JK1976 .N67 2017 (print) | LCC JK1976 (ebook) | DDC 324.6/50973—dc23
LC record available at https://lccn.loc.gov/2016049427

Contents

WHY AMERICAN ELECTIONS ARE FLAWED (AND HOW TO FIX THEM)

Introduction

Like Humpty Dumpty, trust in American elections can be easily damaged, but it is far more difficult to rebuild. The 2016 US presidential elections have highlighted pervasive problems in how American elections work. Secretary Hillary Clinton and Donald Trump battled through exceptionally brutal primary and general election campaigns that have polarized opinions and generated allegations of fraud, vote rigging, repression of voter's rights, and hacking. These procedural concerns did not arise this year, of course; the flaws in the American electoral process have become more apparent over many years. The contemporary tipping point in public awareness occurred during the 2000 Bush-versus-Gore election count. But, like a sagging foundation, several major structural weaknesses have exacerbated doubts in the 2016 campaign, thereby worsening party divisions and further corroding public trust in the electoral process.

It is impossible to fix a problem without understanding its nature. To gather independent evidence about the quality of elections around the world, the Electoral Integrity Project (EIP) was established in 2012, an independent project with a research team based at Harvard and Sydney universities. According to expert estimates developed by EIP, the 2012 and 2014 elections in the United States were the worst among all Western democracies.[1] Without reform, these problems risk damaging the legitimacy of American elections—further weakening public confidence in the major political parties, Congress, and the US government, depressing voter turnout, and exacerbating the risks of contentious outcomes fought through court appeals and public protests.

America is far from alone in its problems at the ballot box; numerous types of flaws and failures undermine elections in developing democracies around the globe. In some, opponents are disqualified. District boundaries are gerrymandered. Campaigns provide a skewed playing field for parties. Independent media are muzzled. Citizens are ill-informed about choices. Balloting is disrupted by bloodshed. Ballot boxes are stuffed. Vote counts are fiddled. Opposition parties withdraw. Contenders refuse to accept the people's choice. Protests disrupt polling. Officials abuse state resources. Electoral registers are out of date. Candidates distribute largesse. Votes are bought. Airwaves favor incumbents. Campaigns are awash with hidden cash. Political finance rules are lax. Incompetent local officials run out of ballot papers.

Incumbents are immune from effective challengers. Rallies trigger riots. Women candidates face discrimination. Ethnic minorities are persecuted. Voting machines jam. Lines lengthen. Ballot box seals break. Citizens cast more than one ballot. Legal requirements serve to suppress voting rights. Polling stations are inaccessible. Software crashes. "Secure" ink washes off fingers. Courts fail to resolve complaints impartially. Each of these problems can generate contentious elections characterized by lengthy court challenges, opposition boycotts, and public demonstrations.[2] In fragile states with a recent history of conflict, electoral failures can trigger further outbreaks of deadly violence and undermine regime legitimacy. The Electoral Integrity Project provides independent evidence from a rolling expert survey to document these problems and monitor how elections vary worldwide.

To understand these issues, the first section describes several major challenges observed during the 2016 US elections, including deepening party polarization over basic electoral procedures, the serious risks of hacking and altering official records, the consequences of deregulating campaign spending, and the lack of federal standards and professional practices in electoral management. To place these issues in broader perspective, Section 2 outlines the core concept and measure of *electoral integrity*, the key yardstick used by the Electoral Integrity Project to evaluate free and fair elections. Section 3 compares cross-national and state-level evidence from expert and mass surveys to diagnose problems in

American elections. Section 4 considers how these challenges could be addressed through several practical steps designed to improve American electoral procedures and practices: establishing secure and convenient voting facilities, improving the independence and professional standards of election management, implementing impartial dispute resolution mechanisms to deal with challenges, and, finally, strengthening accountability and transparency. The conclusion summarizes the core argument and the reforms recommended to advance free and fair elections at home and abroad.

I

Challenges of Electoral Integrity during the 2016 US Elections

The challenges to electoral integrity highlighted by the 2016 US elections are far from new.[1] Several events during the campaign have highlighted long-standing vulnerabilities. Without a comprehensive program of reforms addressing these problems, in a close, heated, and bitterly fought election, the 2016 contest could be a critical "tipping point" triggering lasting harm to its legitimacy. There are many long-standing problems which damage American elections, such as partisan gerrymandering and restrictions on third party ballot access. Five issues are highlighted here as posing growing risks to electoral legitimacy in the 2016 race: partisan polarization over electoral procedures; lack of public confidence following widespread claims of fraud, vote rigging, and the suppression of voter rights; the risks of hacking; the consequences of deregulating campaign funding; and the lack of professional standards of electoral management.

Partisan Polarization over Electoral Procedures

In established democracies, processes for registering and balloting are often regarded today as routine matters, involving largely technical and procedural issues. Reform efforts have commonly focused on practical steps designed to improve administrative and procedural efficiency where there is a broad consensus, such as through the provision of user-friendly online information about the location and opening hours of polling places, ways to strengthen gender equality in elected office, the role of technology in elections, the provision of civic education to strengthen young people's engagement, and the provision of voting facilities for people with disabilities.

In the United States, however, ever since the 2000 Bush-versus-Gore count in Florida, Republican- and Democrat-dominated statehouses have become increasingly polarized over the most appropriate laws for electoral registration and balloting.[2] Like many other issues in contemporary American politics, there is no agreement about what types of reforms should be prioritized to address issues of electoral integrity, including the underlying values of security *versus* inclusiveness. Debate surrounds whether integrity is hurt more by *overly strict* registration and voting procedures (which are thought to cause low turnout, political inequality, greater administrative complexity, and lack of inclusive voting rights by all sectors of society), or by *overly lenient* requirements (which are believed to increase the risks of voter impersonation and thus multiple voting, thereby invalidating legitimate results and damaging public trust). Electoral laws and regulations can be designed to either reduce or raise the logistical barriers (time, effort, and possibly money) which citizens face when seeking to register and/or cast a ballot.[3] These logistical costs reflect one part of the turnout calculus made by the ideal, rational voter, alongside informational costs and calculations of the anticipated benefits arising from participation.[4]

Thus, in Republican-held statehouses, a series of new state laws have sought to tighten voter identification requirements and provide additional verification checks on the accuracy of the electoral register. Proponents argue that these steps help prevent voter impersonation (multiple voting) and thereby strengthen public confidence in the electoral process. Before 2000, fourteen states asked citizens to present an identification document at the polls. In 2013, in *Shelby County v. Holder*, the Supreme Court eviscerated key provisions of the 1965 Voting Rights Act. That law had required fifteen states with a history of discrimination to get the approval of the Justice Department or a federal court before making changes to their voting laws. Since this requirement was abolished, the adoption of voter ID requirements and their stringency accelerated rapidly in GOP-dominated state legislatures such as those in North Carolina, Alabama, and Wisconsin. By 2016, thirty-two states have implemented laws requesting or requiring citizens to show some forms of identification at the polls (see figure 1).[5]

Opponents argue persuasively that claims of voter impersonation and duplicate voting are grossly exaggerated and politically driven.[6] The sporadic cases which do exist are minor, largely due to human error, and insufficient to sway the outcome of an election. Overly stringent requirements may also restrict voters rights, especially disenfranchising mobile populations and sectors of the community lacking the necessary official documents, and thereby serving to intimidate or discriminate against certain types of citizens, especially minority groups, low-income adults, young people, and senior citizens.[7] Making it harder to register and cast a ballot is likely to depress turnout. New regulations also increase the complexities for local officials and poorly trained poll workers when seeking to apply the revised electoral rules correctly. Partisan disagreements have heated up since the passage of new state-level laws and subsequent challenges in the courts.[8] Many (but not all) of the more restrictive attempts have been struck down by the courts as discriminatory, including voting regulations passed in Kansas, North Carolina, North Dakota, Texas, and Wisconsin. Nevertheless, the debate over voting rights and procedures has politicized the electoral process, generated increased

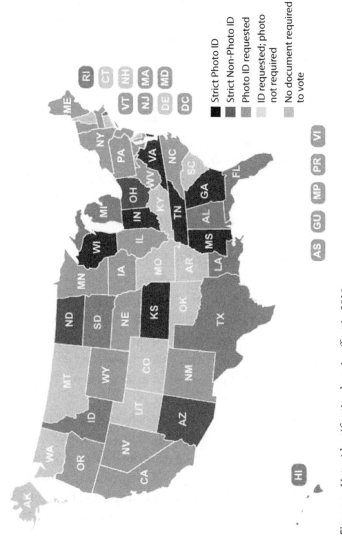

Figure 1: Voter identification laws in effect in 2016

Source: http://www.ncsl.org/research/elections-and-campaigns/voter-id.aspx

Strict Photo ID
Strict Non-Photo ID
Photo ID requested
ID requested; photo not required
No document required to vote

uncertainty and confusion among electoral officials and ordinary citizens about the appropriate requirements needed to register and vote, and probably fueled public mistrust of the process.

By contrast, in seeking to boost turnout, many Democrats have advocated the expansion of "convenience" voting facilities, exemplified by extended hours for voting, the provision of on-demand postal voting, and advance or early-day voting. Those arguing for the loosening of registration procedures contend that such facilities reduce the logistical costs facing citizens who seek to register and cast a ballot, and thereby promote full and equal participation.

Convenience voter *registration* procedures, reducing the time and effort citizens need to be listed on the electoral rolls, are exemplified by online registration, automatic registration, election day registration, pre-qualifying age registration, and rolling registers. In the United States, for example, registration via the Internet has become widely available, with thirty-one states allowing online registration applications in the 2016 elections, although making up only 7 percent of registration submissions.[9]

In addition, convenience *voting* facilities reduce the costs citizens face when casting ballots, including advance voting, assisted voting, overseas voting, absentee balloting, postal voting, extended hours or days, weekend polling, Internet voting, proxy voting, special facilities for the disabled, the production of multi-language informational materials, and the deployment of mobile polling stations.[10] Many states have relaxed the rules to allow any qualified citizen to make use of early and remote balloting without the need to provide a specific reason, such as immobility or travel. Participating through both these types of facilities is particularly important to those with physical disabilities or illnesses, homeworkers responsible for dependents, rural populations living in remote areas, residents in hospitals or retiree communities, military members and expatriates posted abroad, those whose religious commitments prevent them attending polling places on election day, and so on. As a result of implementing these types of provisions, voting in person at a local polling station on election day has become less and less common. According to the Electoral Administration and Voting Survey, for example, in 2014 almost one in four American voters cast their ballot before polling day.[11]

While these reforms may appear to be common-sense and practical steps which serve to strengthen participation in American democracy, critics claim that even well-meaning procedural reforms relaxing legal requirements for the registration and voting process may have unintended consequences: heightening security risks, undermining the secrecy of the ballot, increasing administrative costs and complexities, producing inconsistent and unequal voting rights across America, and thereby possibly, ultimately damaging public confidence in electoral integrity.[12] In other words, it is argued that the desire for inclusive participation needs to be counterbalanced by the need to protect the security of the ballot.[13] In particular, critics charge that overly lax registration and balloting requirements in America have heightened risks of voter impersonation, allowing noncitizens to vote, and other malpractices.[14] In line with these arguments, several Republican-held state houses have sought to overturn convenience voting facilities, catalyzing a series of court challenges. For example, in 2013 North Carolina enacted voter-ID requirements and simultaneously restricted early voting and ended same-day registration, Sunday voting, and pre-registration for teenagers before they turn eighteen. The day the law was signed, the ACLU and the Southern Coalition for Social Justice filed suit on the grounds that the statute discriminated against minority voters in violation of the 14th and 15th Amendments. The lower courts heard these challenges and ruled against the law on the grounds that requirements "target African Americans with almost surgical precision." In August 2016, the US Supreme Court took up the case, upholding the claim that North Carolina's voter ID-provisions were unconstitutional, although all four Republican-nominated justices on the Supreme Court expressed dissent.[15]

Lack of Public Confidence in the Electoral Process

During the 2016 elections, like throwing gasoline on the embers, partisan polarization over these issues has been exacerbated by Donald Trump's repeated claims that the outcome in several battleground states, such as Pennsylvania, is in danger of being "rigged," a serious charge which goes beyond previous Republican claims by implying intentional manipulation of the vote count.[16] Mr. Trump has called for volunteers to sign up as observers in polling places. Credible and experienced monitors can help to ensure that procedures are properly followed, making the process more transparent, without interference.[17] Nevertheless, untrained and inexperienced partisan poll watchers may inflame local tensions and confusion on polling day, disrupting procedures and intimidating citizens. Trump has also claimed that vulnerability to voter impersonation and multiple voting has grown after a series of court decisions threw out many of the more restrictive state voter-ID laws. The 2016 Republican platform urged states to require proof of citizenship and photo ID to prevent abuse of voting procedures.

As I mentioned earlier, the allegations of fraud through pervasive voter impersonation and multiple voting in American elections have been widely discredited; for example, an examination by the Brennan Center for Justice concluded that these problems were exaggerated and largely mythical: "Voter fraud is very rare, voter impersonation is nearly nonexistent, and much of the problems associated with alleged fraud in elections relates to unintentional mistakes by voters or election administrators."[18] The Brennan Center study found 241 potentially fraudulent ballots out of 1 billion ballots cast over a fourteen-year period. Another investigation by News21 for the *Washington Post* found only 2,068 cases of alleged voter fraud had been reported from 2000 to 2012, including only ten cases of voter impersonation.[19]

Contrary to the evidence, however, the heated charges of voter fraud and vote rigging appear to be widely believed among Trump's supporters. If he loses, especially if the final margin of victory is tight, this perception may serve to delegitimize the eventual outcome and fuel protests. Given the media coverage of these Republican accusations, it is hardly surprising that in September 2016 a Gallup poll found that only six in ten Americans were very or fairly confident that their vote would be accurately cast and counted in the US election, down from around three quarters of all Americans a decade earlier.[20] Among Republicans, the proportion of voters who were confident dropped to around half, the lowest that the Gallup poll has ever recorded on this question when asked in a series of surveys. Similarly, a *Washington Post*–ABC News poll of registered voters conducted on September 5–8, 2016 found that nearly half of all Americans (46 percent) believe that voter fraud occurs very or somewhat often, a figure which jumps to two thirds (69 percent) of Trump supporters.[21] At a time of persistently low confidence in American institutions, this deepening erosion of faith in elections is cause for serious concern. Studies have found that citizens often get their information about the integrity of the balloting process from parties; Beaulieu found that party elites provide strong cues for voter perceptions of electoral fraud, producing divergent beliefs among Democrats and Republicans.[22]

The Risks of Hacking Breaches

While myths of multiple voting are largely without foundation, concern about the potential risks of security breaches to the official records have recently become real. The chiefs of the FBI and the National Security Agency regard the potential threat of external attempts to hack the election as serious risks, including the potential threats that are alleged to arise from Russia. Cybersecurity officials believe that Russia-based hackers were behind the break-in to the server of the Democratic National Committee, with the e-mails released to the media the day before the Democratic Convention. Similar reports have circulated e-mails from prominent Republicans such as Colin Powell. Subsequent reports during September 2016 have found evidence of attempts to break into two state registration databases. One incident included stealing information in Illinois from roughly 200,000 voting records. In another attempt, in Arizona, cybercriminals used malware to try to breach voting records, forcing state officials to disable online voting registration for nine days as they investigated the unsuccessful hacking.[23] The aging equipment and vintage software used on many US electronic voting machines, and the lack of sophisticated security to protect state voting records, make these particularly vulnerable to external cyberattack by foreign powers and terrorist groups; many electronic voting machines were purchased by states and counties through a $4 billion federal fund following the Helping America Vote Act of 2002 and never subsequently overhauled or replaced. Official spokespersons suggest that the decentralized nature of US electoral administration provides a partial protection, where security is maintained by 8,000 jurisdictions within states, sometimes by each county, limiting the penetration of efforts by attackers seeking to penetrate the whole system. But this is a weak defense; it would just take minor security breaches to some digital voting registers, electronic voting machines, or software aggregating vote tabulations, in a few local polling places in a couple of swing states, to reduce the credibility of American elections, throw the outcome into chaos, and trigger doubts about the legitimacy of the eventual winner of the presidential contest.[24]

Deregulating Campaign Finance

Along with voters' rights and the security of the process, the issue of campaign finance and checkbook elections has long been a matter of major concern in America—as well as in most countries in the world, as exemplified by major political finance scandals in Italy, Japan, Spain, the United Kingdom, and Brazil.[25] The role of money in politics raises questions about the integrity and transparency of the electoral process, the power of wealthy special interests, and the accountability of elected representatives. In the United States, a series of decisions by the US Supreme Court, including *Citizens United v. the Federal Election Commission* (2010) and *McCutcheon v. FEC* (2014), has dramatically expanded the ability of wealthy individuals, corporations, and groups to spend as much as they like to influence elections.[26] The Center for Responsive Politics estimates that $6 billion will be spent in the 2016 US elections by campaigns, political parties, and corporations hoping to propel their candidates into the White House and what Mark Twain once called the "best Congress money can buy."[27] This would be more than double the amount spent in 2012.

These enduring problems have been highlighted as an issue of public concern during the 2016 campaign, with attacks on the fundraising role of major donors and corporations from both the left (Bernie Sanders) and the right (Donald Trump).[28] Major decisions by the Supreme Court, notably *Citizens United*, have deregulated campaign spending.[29] The growing funding of individual candidates by special interest groups with specific concerns, such as gun rights advocates or environmentalists, has increased polarization by putting pressures on representatives to defend these interests or else risk losing resources.[30] In practice, it remains to be seen how campaign spending develops among the major candidates during the run-up to polling day. In late summer (August 2016), according to FEC figures, Clinton raised more than three times the total funds as compared with Trump ($315 million to around $127 million).[31] At the same time, patterns of spending on campaign communications and local organizations have been upended in this race, with Hillary Clinton outspending Donald Trump in television advertisements by a seventeen-to-one margin in late August.[32] Until Labor Day, Trump relied largely on his substantial advantage in the amount of news coverage contained in free media, as well as the use of social media such as Twitter, and traditional campaign rallies.[33] The role of political finance has caused public concern about the democratic process, and it raises major questions about the weakness of the US Federal Election Commission as the key regulatory agency, which has been gridlocked over reform.

Lack of Professional Standards of Electoral Management

Finally, the issues we have seen during the 2016 US campaign are likely to exacerbate and compound the long-standing lack of a professionalized electoral administration, a feature which has long characterized American contests.[34] Compared with equivalent Western democracies, rather than regulating uniform standards across all polling places and establishing independent and nonpartisan authorities, American elections allow exceptionally partisan control and highly decentralized administrative arrangements. The 2014 report of the bipartisan US Presidential Commission on Election Administration has documented a long series of vulnerabilities. Procedures have been under close scrutiny by the news media ever since the notoriously flawed ballot design in Florida in 2000. Since then, the Commission reported common problems such as wait times in excess of six hours to cast a ballot in Ohio, inaccurate state and local voter registers, insufficiently trained local poll workers, and the breakdown of voting machines in New York; these have continued to put the quality of American elections in the headlines.[35] Standards remain uneven across the country. The Pew Center's 2014 Election Performance Index estimates that states such as North Dakota, Minnesota, and Wisconsin performed relatively well against a range of quality indicators combing voting convenience and electoral integrity, but others, including California, Oklahoma, and Mississippi, demonstrated noticeable shortfalls.[36]

The news media reported a range of problems occurring on polling day during the 2014 midterm elections—some trivial, others more serious—though it remains unclear whether accidental maladministration or intentional dirty tricks were to blame. At least eighteen state election websites were reported to have experienced disruptions on election day, preventing voters from using the sites to locate polling places and ballot information.[37] In Hartford, Connecticut, voters were turned away from polling places that did not open on time due to late-arriving polling lists.[38] The Chicago Board of Election Commissioners reported that more than 2,000 election judges did not turn up at their polling stations after receiving erroneous information from robocalls.[39] In Virginia, a State Department of Elections spokesman said that thirty-two electronic voting machines at twenty-five polling places experienced problems. In both Virginia and North Carolina, there were also claimed cases of electronic polling machines that recorded a vote for the Democratic candidate when the screen was touched to cast a vote for the Republican.[40] The statewide voter registration system crashed in Texas, forcing many to complete provisional ballots when poll workers were unable to confirm voter eligibility.[41] Meanwhile new state laws requiring electors to present photo identification were reported to cause confusion in several states, including Texas, Georgia, and North Carolina.[42]

Among all mature democracies, the nuts and bolts of American contests seem notoriously vulnerable to incompetence and simple human errors arising from the extreme decentralization and partisanship of electoral administration processes.[43] The US Constitution makes state and local officials primarily responsible for administering elections, and the arrangements rely heavily on the partisan appointment of local officials who supervise part-time poll volunteers. In terms of running elections, Article I, Section 4 of the Constitution grants state legislatures the authority to regulate the timing, place, and manner of holding elections for Congress. The state legislatures remain the predominant source of legal regulations for elections, generating a patchwork quilt of complex arrangements even for basic matters such as the hours that polling places are open, the requirements for voter registration and voter identification, and facilities for advance or postal voting.[44] To make it even more complicated, these procedures are then implemented in around 13,000 counties and municipalities across America, where local officials determine practical arrangements such as the location of polling places and ballot designs. Congress has the formal, constitutional authority to "make or alter" state rules, and federal laws governing the right to vote and the regulation of political finance have been progressively weakened or even dismantled by recent court decisions.

In the past, the federal government's power to set election procedures has been limited. Recent concerns about the uneven performance of local and state electoral bodies have prompted some modest federal attempts to improve standards.[45] The Federal Election Commission (FEC) was created in 1974 to regulate and monitor how money is raised and spent in national elections, and to administer public funds in presidential contests. The FEC has strengthened transparency, but over the years it has become an increasingly weak and ineffectual body—the leadership is mired in partisan gridlock and unable to propose reforms with any realistic chance of passing into law. The six-member commission is divided by law so that no more than three commissioners can be members of the same political party and at least four votes are required for any official commission action. In practice this has meant that as Democrat and Republican parties have become increasingly polarized over issues of political finance reform, the commission has been permanently hamstrung during a time when campaigns are awash with money and Supreme Court decisions have loosened major parts of the regulatory framework and donor limits. Even the process of replacing FEC members has become difficult due to the Senate's veto power over presidential nominees.[46] The major decisions deregulating campaign finance have come from a series of rulings by the Supreme Court.

On the other hand, the Florida debacle led to the 2002 Help America Vote Act which created a new national oversight and advisory body, the Electoral Assistance Commission. This body was designed to monitor minimum standards of administrative performance and pool information, but in practice most responsibility for running elections still rests with agencies at state and local levels.[47]

The result of the fragmented and partisan nature of American electoral governance is a bewildering hodgepodge of state laws and local procedures determining some of the most basic electoral procedures and voting rights that vary from place to place, such as the requirements for voter registration, identification in polling places, and casting absentee or advance ballots.[48] Where problems arise, such as Florida in 2000, accountability is diluted across multiple levels of government, and the multiplication of veto-points hinders the introduction of any sweeping procedural reforms. At the same time, states and localities have considerable authority to introduce a variety of new voting procedures, if these are interpreted by the courts as meeting broader constitutional and legal rights.

II

Measuring Electoral Integrity

All these problems suggest that the integrity of American elections is problematic. But much of the debate on this issue remains controversial. The issue of what is to blame for any lack of public trust, whether arising from the risks of insecurity at the ballot or the suppression of voters' rights, remains mired in partisan dispute. Is there more systematic and impartial evidence that can diagnose the problems at the heart of American elections?

Here we can turn to the approach developed by the Electoral Integrity Project, an independent and nonpartisan academic research project established in 2012. EIP defines the idea of electoral integrity as the presence of a set of agreed-upon international conventions and global norms, applying universally to all countries worldwide through the election cycle, including during the pre-election period, the campaign, on polling day, and its aftermath.[1]

For evidence, EIP developed an expert survey of Perceptions of Electoral Integrity (PEI). The method of pooling expert knowledge has been used by many recent studies to measure complex issues that cannot be directly observed, such as by Transparency International's Corruption Perception Index, to assess the risks of malfeasance, and by the Varieties of Democracy project, to estimate trends in democratization. The PEI survey of electoral integrity gathers information covering all independent nation-states around the world that have held direct (popular) elections for the national parliament or presidential elections, excluding micro-states (with populations below 100,000). The 213 elections in 153 nations analyzed in the latest release used in this study, PEI-4.5, fall within the period from July 1, 2012 to June 30, 2016.[2]

For each country, the project identified around forty election experts, defined as a political scientist (or other social scientist in a related discipline) who had demonstrated knowledge of the electoral process in a particular country (such as through publications, membership of a relevant research group or network, or university employment). The selection sought a roughly fifty-fifty balance between international and domestic experts, the latter defined by location or citizenship. Experts were asked to complete an online survey one month after the election. In total, 2,417 completed responses were received in the survey, representing just under one third of the experts that the project contacted (29 percent).

To measure the core concept, the PEI survey questionnaire includes forty-nine items on electoral integrity ranging over the whole electoral cycle. These items fell into eleven sequential sub-dimensions. Most attention in detecting fraud focuses upon the final stages of the voting process, such as the role of observers in preventing ballot-stuffing, vote-rigging, and manipulated results. Drawing upon the notion of a "menu of manipulation," however, the concept of an electoral cycle suggests that failure in even one step in the sequence, or one link in the chain, can undermine electoral integrity, and ultimately democracy.[3]

The overall PEI Index is constructed from imputing missing values and then aggregating these forty-nine items into a 100-point scale. In the United States, further research has expanded the comparison during the 2014 midterm elections, using a similar expert-based survey to estimate and compare the integrity of US states (PEI-US 2014).[4] To monitor public opinion, the 2012 American National Election Study also included a special battery of five items designed to gauge the attitudes of the American electorate toward electoral integrity.

The PEI Index has been tested for external validity (with independent sources of evidence), internal validity (consistency within the group of experts), and legitimacy (how far the results can be regarded as authoritative by stakeholders). The analysis demonstrates substantial external validity when the PEI data are compared with many other expert data-sets, as well as internal validity across the experts within the survey, and legitimacy as measured by levels of congruence between mass and expert opinions within each country.[5] For example, the PEI-4.5 Index is significantly correlated with other standard independent indicators.[6] The PEI Index is the most comprehensive and thorough way to monitor and compare electoral integrity in contests worldwide.

• • • • • • • • • •
• • • • • • • • • •
• • • • • • • • • •

III

Comparing Electoral Integrity within and across States

What does this evidence suggest about the relative performance of US elections when compared with recent elections held in countries worldwide, as well as with similar post-industrial states and Western democracies?

When evaluating the integrity of elections, experts rated America exceptionally poorly. Compared with all 153 countries in the survey, based on the average evaluations of both the 2012 and 2014 US elections, America scored 62 out of the 100-point PEI Index. Compared with the rest of the world, the United States ranks 52nd worldwide. The comparison of countries rated according to the PEI index are illustrated by the global map in figure 2 and regional comparisons in figure 3. Several Nordic welfare states—Denmark, Finland, Norway, and Iceland—consistently lead the world in the

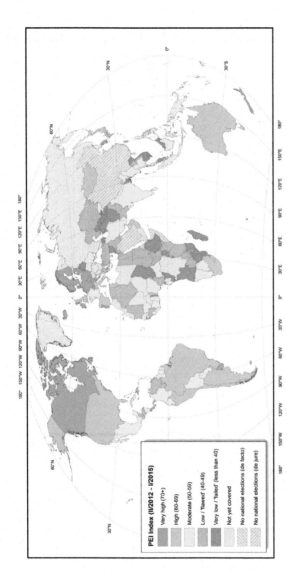

Figure 2: World map of electoral integrity

Note: Mean levels of electoral integrity in national parliamentary and presidential elections from mid-2012 to mid-2016.

Source: The Perceptions of Electoral Integrity expert survey (PEI-4.5), Electoral Integrity Project, www.electoralintegrity project.com

Africa	PEI	Asia-Pacific	PEI	C&E Europe	PEI	Middle East	PEI
Cape Verde*	71	New Zealand	76	Estonia	79	Israel	74
Benin*	69	Republic of Korea	74	Lithuania	77	Tunisia	67
Mauritius	64	Taiwan*	73	Slovenia	77	Oman	60
Rwanda	64	Australia	70	Czech Republic	76	Kuwait	55
South Africa	63	Japan	68	Slovak Republic*	75	Iran*	50
Lesotho	63	Mongolia*	64	Poland	74	Turkey	48
Namibia	60	Vanuatu*	63	Latvia	72	Jordan	46
Ivory Coast	59	Micronesia	61	Croatia	67	Iraq	44
Sao Tome & Principe	58	Bhutan	61	Georgia	59	Egypt	42
Botswana	58	India	59	Moldova	57	Bahrain	38
Ghana	57	Samoa*	57	Bulgaria	56	Afghanistan	32
Sierra Leone	57	Solomon Islands	57	Hungary	56	Syria*	25
Guinea-Bissau	54	Maldives	57	Albania	54		
Nigeria	53	Indonesia	57	Kyrgyzstan	54		
Burkina Faso	53	Myanmar	54	Bosnia	52		
Mali	52	Nepal	54	Serbia*	52		
Central African Rep.	52	Fiji	53	Ukraine	51		
Niger*	52	Singapore	53	Romania	51		
Malawi	48	Philippines*	52	Macedonia	48		
Cameroon	46	Sri Lanka	52	Kazakhstan*	45		
Swaziland	45	Thailand	51	Armenia	44		
Comoros*	45	Pakistan	50	Uzbekistan	39		
Zambia	44	Laos*	48	Turkmenistan	38		
Mauritania	44	Bangladesh	39	Belarus	36		
Tanzania	44	Malaysia	35	Tajikistan	36		
Sudan	43	Vietnam	34	Azerbaijan	35		
Algeria	43	Cambodia	32				
Guinea	42						
Kenya	41						
Madagascar	39						
Togo	38						
Uganda*	37						
Zimbabwe	35						
Angola	35						
Mozambique	35						
Chad*	31						
Djibouti*	29						
Congo, Rep.*	27						
Equatorial Guinea*	25						
Burundi	24						
Ethiopia	23						
Total	47	Total	56	Total	56	Total	48

Figure 3: Electoral integrity by world region

Note: Green = High to Very High Electoral Integrity (PEI Index of 60+); Yellow = Moderate Electoral Integrity (50–59); Red = Low to Very Low Electoral Integrity (less than 50).

Source: The Perceptions of Electoral Integrity expert survey (PEI 4.5) * = updated ratings in 2016

Americas	PEI	Scandinavia	PEI	W. Europe	PEI
Costa Rica	81	Denmark	86	Netherlands	79
Uruguay	75	Finland	86	Switzerland	78
Canada	75	Norway	83	Austria*	77
Brazil	67	Iceland*	82	Portugal*	75
Chile	66	Sweden	81	Belgium	71
Grenada	66			Ireland*	71
Jamaica*	66			Cyprus*	70
Argentina	64			Spain*	69
Barbados	63			Italy	67
United States	62			Greece	66
Peru*	62			Malta	65
Panama	60			United Kingdom	65
Colombia	60				
Mexico	57				
Cuba	56				
Bolivia	55				
Ecuador	55				
Paraguay	55				
El Salvador	54				
Belize	53				
Guyana	53				
Suriname	50				
Guatemala	48				
Venezuela	45				
Honduras	45				
Dominican Rep.*	44				
Haiti	28				
Total	57	**Total**	84	**Total**	71

quality of their elections, as in many other indicators of democratic governance. These countries are followed in the global rankings by Costa Rica (5th), Sweden (6th), Germany (7th), Estonia (8th), the Netherlands (9th), and Switzerland (10th). The fact that many long-established democracies score highly according to the survey suggests that, not surprisingly, historical experience of a long series of multiparty elections is important for their quality. At the same time, however, this is far from an inviolable rule: as well as the United States, some other long-established Western democracies were not well rated, notably the United Kingdom. By contrast many of the newer democracies in the Baltics and post-Communist Europe (such as Estonia, Lithuania, and Slovenia) also performed relatively well, as did Costa Rica and Uruguay in Latin America, Cape Verde and Benin in Africa, and the Republic of Korea in Southeast Asia.

By contrast, countries holding elections scoring *least* well worldwide, ranked in the bottom ten, include Ethiopia (ranked 153rd), Burundi (152nd), Syria (151st), Equatorial Guinea (150th), Republic of Congo (149th), Haiti (148th), Djibouti (147th), Chad (146th), Cambodia (145th), and Afghanistan (144th). Their poor performance reflects the repression of political rights and civil liberties in these countries, as well as common problems of contentious contests flawed by violence, maladministration, and corruption. A more systematic comparison of all 153 countries in the study confirms the impression of the strong association

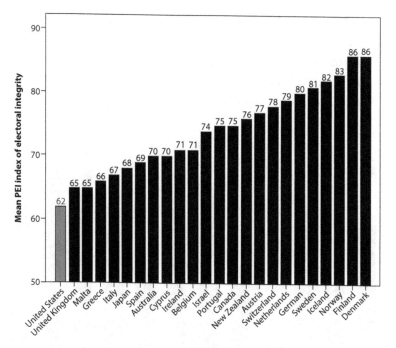

Figure 4: Electoral integrity in twenty-four Western democracies

Note: Mean levels of electoral integrity in national parliamentary and presidential elections from mid-2012 to mid-2016.

Source: The Perceptions of Electoral Integrity expert survey (PEI-4.5), Electoral Integrity Project, www.electoralintegrityproject.com

between the PEI index and democratization (measured by the Freedom House/Polity IV index).[1]

If the comparison is restricted to the two dozen affluent, post-industrial societies and long-established Western democracies with elections in the study, shown in figure 4, the United

States displays the lowest performance in electoral integrity; for example, the United States scored 62 points out of 100, compared with scores in other Anglo-American democracies of 65 in the United Kingdom, 70 in Australia, 75 in Canada, 76 in New Zealand, as well as over 80 in the Scandinavian societies.

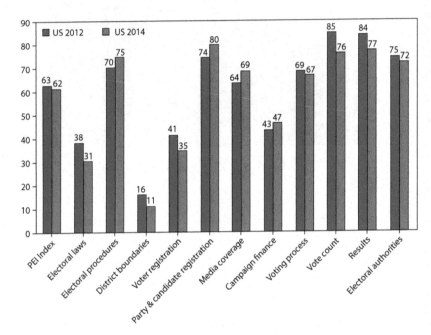

Figure 5: Electoral integrity in the 2012 and 2014 US elections

Note: Mean levels of electoral integrity in the 2012 presidential elections and the 2014 Congressional elections in the United States.

Source: The Perceptions of Electoral Integrity expert survey (PEI-4.5), Electoral Integrity Project, www.electoralintegrityproject.com

To see whether these estimates remain robust, comparisons can also be drawn between the 2012 US Presidential elections and the 2014 US Congressional elections. Given the limited number of experts assessing each case, relatively modest differences across elections should not be exaggerated. Nevertheless, as shown in figure 5, according to the two expert surveys, there are broadly similar assessments across both contests, but some dimensions are rated marginally worse in 2014, including electoral laws and voter registration (probably reflecting the increasingly controversial debate in statehouses and courtrooms), district boundaries, the vote count, and results. The evidence does not suggest that the quality of American elections has improved over these successive contests; if anything, problems are perceived to have worsened.

To analyze the weakest links during the electoral cycle, figure 6 illustrates the PEI scores by each of the eleven stages in the United States compared with other similar Anglo-American democracies. The results suggest that, compared with these countries, US elections raised the greatest concerns among experts about electoral laws, voter registration, the process of drawing district boundaries, as well as the regulation of campaign finance.[2]

Finally, are these problems perceived just by technical election experts, or do these flaws matter also for ordinary citizens and the general public? Evidence from the sixth wave of the World Values Survey demonstrates that electoral integrity often has important consequences for public trust and confidence

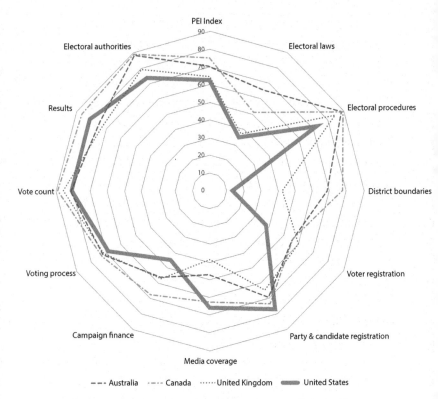

Figure 6: Electoral integrity by stages in Anglo-American democracies

Note: Mean levels of electoral integrity in national parliamentary and presidential elections from mid-2012 to mid-2016.

Source: The Perceptions of Electoral Integrity expert survey (PEI-4.5), Electoral Integrity Project, www.electoralintegrityproject.com

in the electoral process and institutions, support for democracy, civic engagement, and political representation.[3] By contrast, where citizens believe that widespread malpractices have occurred—whether falsely or correctly—then this corrodes citizens' trust in the electoral process, political parties, parliaments and governments, and their confidence in democracy, depresses voter turnout and civic engagement, and thereby undermines channels of political representation.[4] In established democracies, minor malpractices can often be remedied through legal and administrative reforms to electoral institutions and voting procedures without undermining support for the regime or destabilizing the state. In more challenging contexts, however, such as in transitional regimes, divided societies emerging from conflict, and fragile states, simple minor flaws—or even major failures in elections—can have a far more serious impact by potentially fueling social instability, riots, and violence in contentious elections, undermining fragile gains in democratization and triggering popular uprisings and intercommunal conflict seeking revolutionary change.[5]

Evaluating the Electoral Performance of American States

The 2016 campaign saw multiple complaints about how American elections work. To evaluate performance, following the election the Electoral Integrity Project conducted an expert survey of Perceptions of Electoral Integrity across all fifty US states and Washington, DC. The research gathered evaluations from 726 political scientists based in local universities in each state. Respondents were asked to evaluate electoral integrity in their own state two weeks after polling day. Given the diversity of issues, the survey used an identical instrument to the global survey, using the same forty-nine core indicators. Election experts were asked to judge a wide range of issues, such as whether elections in their state were well managed, votes were counted fairly, and newspapers provided balanced election news, without any reference to political parties or the party in control of the state house. The responses were then grouped into eleven categories reflecting all stages throughout the electoral cycle, during the pre-election, campaign, polling day, and its aftermath. Several characteristics of states were also gathered, such as the partisan composition of state legislatures, the share of the vote in the 2016 presidential race, and the marginality of the contest. Details about the individual experts were also gathered, such as their age, sex, and ideological positions, to see whether these characteristics were systematically associated with evaluations of electoral integrity.

Is the data reliable? It can be argued that political scientists are not neutral judges, given the well-known academic bias toward supporting liberal democratic values. Indeed, the whole idea of independent "experts" has come under dispute in this populist and hyper-partisan age. But the external validity of the Perceptions of Electoral Integrity Index has been widely tested in previous research and found to be strongly correlated with other standard sources of evidence, like the Varieties of Democracy project, Freedom House, and Polity IV. It is important to be cautious when interpreting absolute rankings since differences between states were often relatively modest and the number of responses was limited in some states, such as Utah and North Dakota, although none of these are in the worst performing cases. Finally, the survey measures expert *Perceptions* of Electoral Integrity, taken as both a proxy for the underlying phenomena and as important construction of social reality in its own right.

The results supplement other sources of evidence which will become available in due course, including comparison of state performance indices (such as voting wait times and turnout rates), the forensic analysis of precinct-level voting statistics, scrutiny of credible complaints and legal cases, surveys of poll-workers and local electoral officials, analysis of social media, and surveys of public opinion.

Ranking Electoral Integrity and Malpractices across US States

Experts evaluated the 2016 elections across all fifty US states and Washington, DC. The results show that the south remains the region of America which experts assess as having the weakest electoral performance. The Supreme

Court ruled that voting restrictions in the South were a bygone problem, eliminating Section 5 of the Voting Rights Act, which had required states with a history of racial discrimination to get Department of Justice approval before changing voting laws. Evidence from these expert evaluations, and from recent GOP State House shenanigans in North Carolina to restrict the power of the governor before Democrat Roy Cooper takes over, suggests that this may have been unduly optimistic. Rust belt "Blue Wall" states were also seen as problematic. By contrast experts assessed the quality of elections more positively in the Pacific West and New England.

But state performances varied even within major regions. Overall, states scoring as worst in the perceptions of electoral integrity index in this election were Arizona (ranked last), followed by Wisconsin, Tennessee, Oklahoma, and Mississippi. Several of these states had also been poorly rated previously in the 2014 Pew Election Performance Index. By contrast, the US states that experts rated most highly in electoral integrity were Vermont, Idaho, New Hampshire, and Iowa.

The exact reasons underlying varying performance still need probing further. Problems can arise at any stage of the electoral process—not just at the ballot box. To dive deeper into the data, we can look at how experts evaluated state performance across each of the eleven stages of the 2016 contest. The results show that the stages of the vote count, the voting process, and the role of electoral authorities have a fairly clean bill of health across nearly all US states. By contrast, however, according to experts, far greater weakness in many American states concern the stages of district boundary delimitation, state electoral laws, campaign media, and political money.

Clearly some of these issues are already on the mainstream reform agenda. Allegations of voter fraud received massive attention and the reform of state electoral laws was also widely discussed in the campaign, following the passage of several restrictive voting and registration procedures that were subsequently struck down by the courts, such as in North Carolina. The need to reform the role of money in politics was covered during the campaign, including playing a big part of Bernie Sanders' campaign. Donald Trump's populist rhetoric also railed against corruption in politics, including the nefarious role of beltway lobbyists and self-interested members of Congress. In terms of campaign communications, the impact of fake news and Russian meddling in the campaign have both emerged as major issues of bipartisan concern after November 8, despite some poo-pooing by Trump.

By contrast, there are other broader issues about campaign media that should raise serious concern, as reports by Harvard's Shorenstein Center have highlighted, including the lack of substantive policy discussion during the campaign, the false equivalency standards of journalism, and the overwhelmingly negative tone of news coverage.

Moreover, the issue of gerrymandered district boundaries, regarded by experts as the worst aspect of US voting procedures, was never seriously debated throughout the campaign. The practice ensures that representatives are returned time and again based on mobilizing the party faithful, without having to appeal more broadly to constituents across the aisle, thus exacerbating the bitter partisanship which plagues American politics. Gerrymandering through GOP control of state legislatures has also led to a systematic pro-Republican advantage in House districts, which is likely to persist at least until 2022. In 2016 House Republicans won 241 seats out of 435 (55 percent), although they won only 49.1 percent of the popular vote, a six-percentage point winner's bonus.

Where Malpractices Occurred, Were They in States Won by Trump or Clinton?

So how far does the performance of states relate to party control of state legislatures? We can compare expert assessments of each of the stages during the electoral cycle with which party controlled the State House. The results clearly demonstrate that, according to the expert evaluations, Democratic-controlled states usually had significantly greater electoral integrity than Republican-controlled states, across all stages except one (the declaration of the results, probably reflecting protests in several major cities following the unexpected Trump victory). The partisan gap was substantial and statistically significant on the issues of gerrymandered district boundaries, voter registration, electoral laws, and the performance of electoral officials.

Given this pattern, not surprisingly there was a tendency for Trump to win more states with electoral malpractices, while Clinton won more states with electoral integrity. We do not claim, as we do not have sufficient evidence, that Trump won these states *because* of malpractices. But the correlation is clear. Thus, throughout the campaign, and even afterwards, it was Donald Trump who repeatedly claimed that the election was rigged and fraudulent. In terms of votes being intentionally cast illegally, the strict meaning of "voter fraud." there is little or no evidence supporting these claims. But if the idea of integrity is understood more broadly, there is indeed evidence from this study that US elections suffer from several systematic and persistent problems—and Donald Trump and the Republican party appear to have done well in states with the most problems.

To see whether perceptions of electoral integrity matter for American voters, we can turn to the 2012 American National Election Survey, the standard study of voting behavior in the United States, where the post-election wave contained several items using four-point scales to monitor how ordinary citizens assessed electoral integrity in the United States, including whether they approved or disapproved of the fairness of electoral officials, the fairness of media coverage of the campaign, whether votes were counted fairly, whether voters

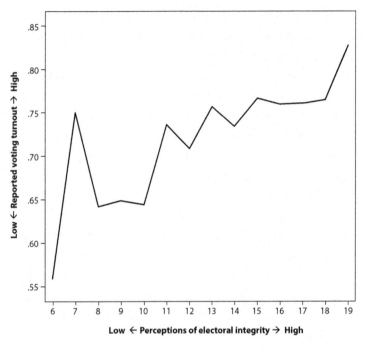

Figure 7: American perceptions of electoral integrity and voting turnout

Source: American National Election study 2012

have genuine choice, and whether rich people buy elections. These items were highly intercorrelated so they were used to form a summary twenty-point index of electoral integrity.[6] The results of the multivariate analysis confirmed that American perceptions of electoral integrity predicted significantly lower levels of reported voting turnout, even after controlling for several standard factors that are also associated with participation, including educational qualifications, age, sex, race, support for the winning presidential candidate and political interest. As shown in figure 7, those with greater confidence in the integrity of the American electoral process were far more likely to vote. By contrast, as in many other countries, those citizens doubting the fairness of how elections worked were far more likely to stay home. Given that US turnout has long been among the lowest in Western democracies, typically about ten to twenty points below equivalent European societies, it is vital to improve the integrity of elections.

IV

What Is to Be Done?

By all these indicators, therefore, the evidence points to a range of enduring problems in American elections. Most attempts to strengthen US elections involve piecemeal reforms, often worthwhile but technical in nature.[1] These are equivalent to rearranging the deckchairs on the *Titanic*. Instead, what is needed is a more comprehensive wholesale plan addressing systematic and structural weaknesses at the heart of American elections. Several steps are recommended, illustrated in figure 8, including a sequential process involving improving legal regulations, building the capacity of administrative agencies such that these laws can be implemented efficiently and effectively, monitoring performance, and strengthening accountability and oversight. These are the initiatives commonly used in many countries around

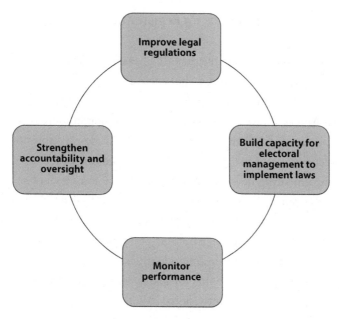

Figure 8: Recommended sequence of reforms

the world where electoral assistance seeks to improve electoral integrity.[2] In practice, perhaps the most urgent practical steps in the United States involve: (i) reforming electoral regulations for registration and balloting; (ii) building more impartial, independent, and professional electoral management bodies; (iii) monitoring performance and expanding transparency through electoral observers, developing comparative and state-level indicators, and strengthening watchdog agencies; (iv) strengthening dispute resolution mechanisms and oversight agencies.

(i) Legal Regulations for Registration and Balloting

The first step is to overhaul the basic regulation of registration and balloting, the source of so much controversy in US elections. The state laws that govern these processes in America have come under scrutiny, although there is no consensus about the importance of the trade-off values of security versus inclusiveness, as well as the consequences of implementing new regulations. There is a complex hodge-podge of practices. Many states have sought to expand convenience voting, including facilities such as election-day registration; online registration; pre-registration (prior to attaining the age of 18); voter identification requirements to cast a ballot; voting rights for felons; absentee ballots; mail ballots; early ballots; provisional ballots; publication of voter leaflets; and publication and distribution of sample ballots. The National Conference of State Legislatures (NCSL) Election Laws database contains information on the election laws and procedures used in all fifty states ranging from voter identification requirements to methods of disseminating voter information.[3]

Are these measures effective? As discussed earlier, by reducing the logistical costs, the hope is the measures will boost turnout. Yet they do nothing to alter the other informational costs involved in voting, nor do they address the issue of genuine choice at the ballot box. Nevertheless, considerable research about the effects of these initiatives has been conducted, often by focusing on the effect of introducing reforms into particular states, such as the use of all-postal voting in Oregon, or across American states, with some work in several other established democracies, such as the United Kingdom and Switzerland.[4] Despite the extensive body of literature, it still remains difficult to establish conclusively the effects of any single type of electoral law on participation, not least because multiple factors affect turnout.[5]

In one of the seminal early studies on convenience voting, Rosenstone and Wolfinger concluded that US states that used the most relaxed registration processes had higher turnout, and their research suggests that similar effects would follow by lowering the costs of registration elsewhere in the country.[6] Similarly, Piven and Cloward have argued that legal-institutional factors, including registration procedures, are the most important barriers to voting participation for disadvantaged groups in America.[7] Burden et al. find that while election-day registration has a positive effect on participation, another convenience measure, early voting, actually tended to depress turnout.[8] So while most empirical studies find that stricter registration and balloting rules do correlate with lower turnout, at the same time, reforms designed to ease the process do not necessarily boost participation substantially.[9]

US states like Minnesota, with strong participatory cultures, are also most likely to adopt lenient registration laws, such as election day registration. As a result, it may be misleading to extrapolate from these contexts to assume that similar effects would arise from exporting lenient registration facilities to other states, like Alabama, with more restrictive traditions of voter rights.[10] Convenience voting facilities are most often used by engaged citizens, reinforcing their propensity to vote, but this may thereby exacerbate any social gaps in turnout arising from age, socioeconomic status, education, ethnicity, or sex.[11] Additionally, critics claim that well-meaning procedural reforms making legal requirements for the registration and voting process more lenient may also have unintended consequences, such as through heightening security risks, undermining the secrecy of the ballot, increasing administrative costs and complexities, producing inconsistent and unequal voting rights across America, and thereby possibly ultimately damaging public confidence in electoral integrity.[12] Elsewhere, for examples in the United Kingdom, the introduction of online registration, while seen as part of the common-sense drive to modernize elections, has also had consequences by making the system more vulnerable to fraud.[13]

In short, the desire for inclusive participation needs to be counterbalanced by the need to protect the security of the ballot.[14] The introduction of electoral reforms introducing convenience voting is useful as a straightforward "fix" for low turnout, and the results may be positive, but in practice, new facilities also need to protect the security of the ballot. Thus convenience and security are not either/or tradeoff values, but they should ideally be combined.

As discussed earlier, many other states have sought to implement stricter photo IDs for registration and voting, a process that could be straightforward if photo IDs were free and provided by state and federal agencies. For example, in India, which is a vast and complex developing country and federal state containing over 800 million people, all Indian citizens who qualify to vote are provided by the Indian Electoral Commission with free photo IDs that are matched to identical photo records listed against all names on the electoral register. The card also serves as general identity proof, address proof, and age proof for casting votes as well as for other purposes such as buying a mobile phone SIM card or applying for a passport. If India can do this, in the days of smart credit cards and digital payments through smartphones, then such a measure should not be beyond the capacity of the US federal government. And this is only one dimension of improving secure voting records—electronic machines that do not leave a paper trail also need replacing, and digital voting records must have overhauled security against hacking. All these steps would strengthen public confidence in the integrity of the electoral process and undermine the legitimate criticisms of convenience voting.

(ii) Building Independent, Impartial and Professional Electoral Management

Passing new laws and regulations is only the first step. They require the capacity for local officials and poll workers to implement them in an impartial and uniform manner. Indeed, electoral officials are the front-line agencies implementing electoral integrity.

These officials should ideally meet several general guiding principles and values that are common in public sector management and that are thought to ensure legitimate and credible processes and outcomes meeting international standards. These principles include de facto *independence* from undue interference in their activities from the executive branch or partisan forces, *integrity* so that the process is free of fraud and corruption, *transparency* to build trust in the accuracy and honesty of the process, *efficiency* so that services are delivered effectively, equitably, and within budget, *impartiality* so that officials are not biased toward any single contestant, and *professionalism* so that staff have the training, expertise, and resources to manage tasks well.[15] Similar principles are echoed in many of the practical guidelines designed to strengthen electoral administration, such as by International IDEA, IFES, and the OSCE.

The organizational structure, legal mandate, and administrative functions of electoral agencies vary substantially from one country to another. So does their de facto autonomy, which is dependent on their constitutional and legal status, their scope and mandate, provisions for the nomination, appointment, and removal of senior members, the capacity for external actors and other branches of government to overrule the agency's decisions and oversee its operations, and the body's financial independence. The primary models of electoral administration, however, concern whether the main actors are governmental or independent agencies (on the horizontal axis) and whether decision-making and regulations are largely centralized or localized (on the vertical). Based on these distinctions, US electoral administration is primarily governmental-localized. This is quite possibly the worst combination. It maximizes the opportunities for partisan interests *and* lack of uniform standards, generating a multitude of problems.

Decentralized and partisan agencies. In the United States, electoral administration has traditionally been handled at a highly decentralized level. The American constitution gives state and local officials primary responsibilities for administering elections. The system relies on partisan local officials who, in turn, supervise poorly trained poll volunteers. As mentioned earlier, constitutional requirements limit the US federal government's role in elections, but this role has expanded somewhat amid growing concern for the performance of local and state electoral bodies; these concerns led to the 2002 Help America Vote Act and establishment of the bipartisan US Election Assistance Commission.[16]

The decentralized structure hinders the implementation of effective electoral reforms across the whole country, such as establishing uniform opening times for polling places, professional training programs for managers and poll workers, more uniform standards for equipment, and a one-stop shop providing citizens with information about where and how to register and vote. People's basic right to register and their opportunities to vote should not vary according to whether they happen to live in Texas, North Carolina, Oregon, or Massachusetts. A more independent and less partisan agency could reduce partisan interests and improve professional standards of electoral administration.

This contrasts with many established democracies where central authorities are responsible for managing and overseeing elections. In the government model, those units are typically located in the Ministry of Interior, Ministry of Justice, Home Office, or equivalent department of state. This arrangement persists today in several European states, such as the Swedish Electoral Authority, the German Ministry of Interior, the Swiss Federal Chancellery, and the Norwegian Ministry for Local Government and Regional Development. In these countries, the civil service has a general reputation for professional neutrality and impartiality. Among all countries worldwide, International IDEA estimates that around one quarter continue to use the governmental model for running elections.[17] In this model, unlike in the United States, a fair degree of centralization ensures professional standards and uniform practices operate across the whole country, such as on basic matters of voter registration and balloting procedures, with accountability to the national legislature. The unit located within a central government department is typically responsible for administering elections, staffed by permanent civil servants, and headed by a cabinet minister who is directly accountable to the legislature, and thus indirectly to the electorate.

Where election management bodies (EMBs) under the governmental model exist at national level, they are usually led by a minister or civil servant and they are answerable to a cabinet minister. With very few exceptions they have no "members." Their budget falls within a government ministry and/or under local authorities.[18] This model persists in several European countries.[19] The day-to-day administration of elections, such as maintaining voter registries, organizing balloting, running polling places, and counting ballots, is devolved to government authorities at provincial, state, municipal, and constituency levels operating under uniform regulations and voting rights. The national parliament retains the primary prerogative of lawmaking, establishing the statutory framework of electoral regulations. Regional and local officials are responsible for the detailed application and implementation of these procedures in each locality, and the courts for interpreting the laws and adjudicating disputes.

One additional potential advantage of the governmental-centralized model is that electoral authorities in many democracies such as the United Kingdom can call upon the existing resources of the public sector to run elections, including commonly deploying the permanent pool of skilled, experienced, and trained full-time employees at national and local authority levels to administer contests. Electoral authorities can also use the existing technological and communication infrastructure of national and local governments, as in the United Kingdom, reducing overhead costs and the duplication of services. In democratic states, the model also provides a clear chain of accountability for any errors that arise. Local government staff are supervised by national electoral officials who are, in turn, accountable to a government minister and thus ultimately subject to parliamentary oversight and the general electorate.

The aforementioned US Electoral Assistance Commission (EAC) was established in 2002 in reaction to the Florida debacle, and strengthening and expanding its role and mandate would be one important way to improve uniform standards across America.[20] Other federal states, like Canada and Australia, have a one-stop shop for coordinating standards of electoral management, and the United States could usefully learn from these experiences while still allowing local bodies to implement these standards.

At the same time, however, the main danger is that where electoral administration is the responsibility of civil servants working in central ministries or local authorities, and thus subject to executive control and legislative oversight, the process is thought vulnerable to either the actual or the perceived abuse of power and the risk of manipulation to benefit the interests of the governing party or parties. This is particularly dangerous in states with predominant parties, fragmented opposition parties, and weak parliamentary and judicial oversight of the executive. Electoral officials need to be impartial and independent of government or other external influences from political parties, special interests, or the military if the process and results are to be trusted as credible, transparent, and fair. What works in Sweden, Belgium, and Denmark may therefore be far from appropriate in newer democracies that also have a governmental model of electoral administration.

Independent administrative agencies. Today two-thirds of all countries have established an independent administrative agency that is legally separate from government to manage elections (found in 131 countries out of 187 independent nation-states worldwide or 70 percent).[21] On the vertical axis, these institutions can also be highly centralized, where most key decisions are taken by a commission or agency with nationwide authority to regulate and manage lower levels of governance, or they may be highly decentralized, allowing local counties and states/provinces to determine their own arrangements.

Recent years have seen several post-industrial countries adopting new public sector management reforms where several government functions are transferred from central departments of state to specific administrative and regulatory agencies in the public sector.[22] In several Anglo-American countries, including New Zealand, the United Kingdom, and Australia, in recent decades the tendency has been to establish more specialized central agencies for managing elections, thereby delegating responsibility for public services that used to be the province of large bureaucratic ministries. Similar trends have been observed in Canada, France, and the Netherlands, although they are thought to be less marked in Belgium, Finland, Germany, and Sweden.[23] Independent regulatory and administrative agencies have been established in the public sector to provide delegated authority over many policy areas, such as environmental protection, food safety, pharmaceuticals, and telecoms. It is widely believed that this separation of specialized agencies from direct government control avoids political interference and potential conflicts of interest, as well as being more efficient, and thus strengthens the delivery of goods and services in the public interest.[24]

Reflecting this development, many countries have transferred responsibilities for election management from government departments to legally independent administrative agencies, with chief executives composed of experts or partisan members, which operate at arm's length from the executive. The name of these bodies varies in different countries and they are often called electoral commissions, electoral tribunals, electoral boards, electoral courts, departments of elections, election institutes or election councils, and so on, known generically as election management bodies

(EMBs).[25] Agency models of electoral administration create "arms-length" separation from the government through the mechanism of establishing de jure formal legal independence. The agency model has often been established to run the first elections following regime transitions, such as the National Election Commission in Poland, the Independent Election Commission in South Africa, and the Central Election Bureau in Romania. The model has also become increasingly popular among established democracies; for example, through agencies such as the Australian Electoral Commission (since 1984) and the UK Electoral Commission (since 2000). This type of arrangement is described by International IDEA as those where "elections are organized and managed by an EMB which is institutionally independent and autonomous from the executive branch of government, and which has and manages its own budget." Under the independent model, an EMB is not accountable to a government ministry or department. It may be accountable to the legislature, the judiciary, or the head of state. EMBs under the independent model may enjoy varying degrees of financial autonomy and accountability, as well as varying levels of performance accountability. They are composed of members from outside the permanent civil service.[26]

The main advantage of the agency model is that by insulating electoral officials from outside pressures, this helps to curb any potential conflict of interest, partisan meddling, and the abuse of power by external forces, especially where it is suspected that the electoral arbitrator is biased toward incumbent politicians, political parties, the governing party, or powerful elites. By delegating responsibility for electoral administration to independent agencies, politicians agree to abide by the rules, strengthening the credibility of the electoral process.[27] The importance of independence is a prevalent perspective within the international community, for example a recent report for Elections Canada emphasizes: "Most election officers and scholars regard independence as the single most crucial test of the soundness of electoral governance arrangements."[28] The major risk of concentrating responsibilities in the hands of elected officials is that decisions are more easily manipulated by the party or parties controlling the executive, for example if the outcome of a contest threatens the power of incumbent elites.

There are many important variations in these arrangements across countries, however, especially in degree of centralization and local decentralization, reflecting long-standing contrasts between unitary and federal states. The United States, in particular, remains exceptional compared with most other long-standing democracies in its high degree of partisanship and decentralization. Yet regulatory policies and administrative procedures are less coherent if decision-making is dispersed across multiple independent national agencies, weakening coordinated or "joined-up" governance, for example if separate specialist bodies are established for the regulation of campaign broadcasting, the allocation of political finance, party registration, and boundary delimitation. With the decentralization of decision-making to local authorities, basic procedures, such as the hours polling stations are open, or the qualifications and application processes to be included on the electoral register, vary from one locality to another and thus citizens' fundamental voting rights are not consistently applied across all jurisdictions. Some poorly resourced local agencies, which have suddenly to ramp up efforts to run contests at periodic intervals, may lack the professional experience, permanent personnel, and technical machinery to manage these tasks well. Decentralization giving more discretion to local electoral officials also expands the number of entry points and thus the potential risks of corruption and malfeasance. If problems arise, it remains more difficult to establish "where the buck stops" among multiple agencies with overlapping functions, weakening accountability. For example, even if both Democrats and Republicans agree that there should not be excessively long lines at polling stations, it remains difficult to implement straightforward solutions in the United States, such as those suggested by the presidential commission, due to the dispersed authorities of the state and local bodies running elections.[29] Therefore structural reforms to the process of electoral management should be considered in the United States, at minimum strengthening the roles of the FEC and EAC and promoting more autonomous regulatory agencies with uniform professional standards.

(iii) Monitoring Performance

In general, attempts at monitoring electoral integrity are part of a broader set of initiatives concerning governance transparency and accountability. These qualities are generally thought to help plug the leaky pipes of corruption and inefficiency, channel government spending more efficiently, and produce better public services. In the field of electoral governance, greater openness about the rules and procedures, outcomes, and decisions processes used by electoral authorities is widely assumed to build public trust, improve policy-making, and facilitate accountability.[30] By revealing problems, it is generally believed that the reports published by election observers, the news media, and citizen watchdog groups will pressure electoral officials and elected representatives to implement reforms and deter malpractice in future contests. By contrast, in the words of the Open Society Institute: "Silence and secrecy are two of the most powerful tools that governments can employ to mute critics and cloak their actions from public scrutiny."[31] Even if unable to generate positive benefits, there is still a presumption in favor of open electoral governance since, by contrast, "the absence of transparency in electoral processes invariably leads to the suspicion that fraudulent activities are taking place."[32] On whether disclosure alone has the capacity to deliver major benefits, however, it seems unlikely unless it is also coupled with other reforms that improve the professional standards of electoral administration and reduce the role of partisan interests.[33]

(iv) Improving Federal Oversight and Dispute Resolution Mechanisms

The judiciary has traditionally played an active role in determining whether new state laws governing voting rights and electoral procedures meet constitutional standards, including striking out many of the most recent attempts to introduce strict voter photo identification requirements.[34] The courts, rather than the legislative branch, have also arguably played the most important role in determining contemporary campaign finance regulations. In *Bush v. Gore*, 531 U.S. 98, in 2000, the rulings by the Supreme Court essentially determined the outcome of the race, allowing George W. Bush's victorious Florida electoral college votes to stand.[35] Without a replacement for Justice Antonin Scalia, the Supreme Court composition remains evenly divided in 2016. The danger, therefore, is that any legal appeals arising from the November 2016 elections, such as allegations of local voting irregularities or malfeasance, could be deadlocked. The divisive nature of the issues may leave the eight justices unable to decide who can cast the ballots that will determine control of the White House and Congress. In a closely fought and highly polarized race, in particular, disputes that are unable to be decided by the courts could well serve to delegitimize the outcome.

In many other countries, however, special courts and mediation processes are often established in advance to deal with any electoral disputes and problems that arise throughout all stages of the electoral cycle. The aim is to deal with complaints in a timely, just, and impartial manner, avoiding partisan conflict, upholding rights, and facilitating acceptance of the eventual result by all sides in any dispute. Effective systems of electoral justice safeguard the legality of the process and the rights of citizens, promote consensus, and strengthen the legitimacy of the process. Electoral Dispute Resolution Systems, which are independent of electoral management bodies, take different institutional forms in different countries, as described in a comprehensive global handbook published by International IDEA, but the core idea is now widely accepted. The United States could learn from these practices.[36]

V

Conclusions and Recommendations

In conclusion, considerable evidence suggests that problems in the American electoral process have worsened, and piecemeal reforms won't be enough to compensate for growing party polarization and declining public confidence, both of which have risen since 2000. Events during the 2016 campaign have deepened the fractures in public trust. The idea of system support by David Easton suggests that many people may be critical of elected leaders and representatives, as well as the way that representative institutions work.[1] But this, by itself, can be regarded as a healthy process that does not necessarily undermine the public's faith in democracy.[2] If the public becomes skeptical of the game's basic rules, however, and there is little agreement about how elections should function in any state, and sore losers are willing to throw around cavalier accusations of fraud and vote rigging, then this is far more likely to trigger a genuine legitimacy crisis in American democracy. The consequences of such a crisis are far deeper and more damaging than the events in Florida's 2000 election. Time will tell whether future US elections work smoothly or encounter major problems. But in close and highly polarized contests, with diverse practices of electoral administration heavily reliant upon the local decisions of partisan officials, despite the best efforts of poorly trained poll workers, American elections are risky enterprises where outcomes may be determined by the legal wisdom of the courts rather than a count of the votes cast in the ballot box.

Several major challenges face US elections, including deepening party polarization over electoral procedures, the risks that electronic records are open to hacking, and the effects of deregulating campaign spending, all compounded by the lack of professional standards of electoral management. Evidence from expert surveys suggests that, although some cries of fraud are politically driven and without foundation, there is a rational basis for concern. Cries of wolf are common, but this does not mean that alarm is without foundation. The evidence shows that recent US elections display the worst performance among two dozen Western democracies.

Policy reforms designed to strengthen US electoral laws and procedures include electoral reforms designed to build independent and impartial electoral management bodies, develop better dispute resolution mechanisms, and strengthen transparency and accountability mechanisms. Matters of electoral governance should not be determined through laws enacted by self-interested partisan representatives in state houses—the equivalent to putting the fox in charge of the chicken coop. Instead, the reform process needs to engage us all. By themselves, the proposed reforms will not automatically restore confidence in elections overnight, but they are the first step in the long-term process of stemming the loss of public trust in American elections.

Acknowledgments

The study is drawn from the Electoral Integrity Project (EIP), an independent research project focused on why elections fail and what can be done about it. All details are at www.electoralintegrityproject.com. The EIP project is based at Harvard University's John F. Kennedy School of Government and the Department of Government and International Relations at the University of Sydney. Research has been generously supported by the award of the Kathleen Fitzpatrick Australian Laureate from the Australian Research Council, as well as grants from International IDEA, Global Integrity, the Australian Research Council, the Association of World Electoral Bodies (A-WEB), and (at Harvard) by the Weatherhead Center for International Affairs, the Roy and Lila Ash Center for Democratic Governance and

Innovation, and the Australian Studies Committee. The study would not have been possible without the assistance of the research team—Ferran Martinez i Coma, Richard W. Frank, Max Grömping, Jeffrey Karp, Alexandra Kennett, Alessandro Nai, and Andrea Abel van Es—as well as all the fellows and interns visiting the project.

Notes

Introduction

1 See Pippa Norris, Ferran Martínez i Coma, Alessandro Nai, and Max Grömping, *The Year in Elections, 2014* (Sydney: The Electoral Integrity Project, University of Sydney, 2015).

2 Pippa Norris, Richard Frank, and Ferran Martinez i Coma, "Contentious Elections: From Votes to Violence," in *Contentious Elections: From Ballots to Barricades*, ed. Frank Norris and Ferran Martinez i Coma (New York: Routledge, 2015).

I. Challenges of Electoral Integrity during the 2016 US Elections

1 See, for example, Bruce E. Cain, Todd Donovan, and C. J. Tolbert, *Democracy in the States: Experimentation in Election*

Reform (Washington, DC: Brookings Institution Press, 2008); Brian L. Fife, *Reforming the Electoral Process in America* (Santa Barbara, CA: Praeger, 2010); Michael J. Hanmer, *Discount Voting: Voter Registration Reforms and Their Effects* (New York: Cambridge University Press, 2009); Martha Kropf and David C. Kimball, *Helping America Vote: The Limits of Election Reform* (New York: Routledge, 2011); R. Michael Alvarez, Lonna Atkeson, and Thad E. Hall, eds., *Confirming Elections: Creating Confidence and Integrity through Election Auditing* (New York: Palgrave Macmillan, 2012); Barry C. Burden and Charles Stewart III, eds., *The Measure of American Elections* (New York: Cambridge University Press, 2014); R. Michael Alvarez and Bernard Grofman, *Election Administration in the United States* (New York: Cambridge University Press, 2014).

2   Richard L. Hasen, *The Voting Wars: From Florida 2000 to the Next Election Meltdown* (New Haven: Yale University Press, 2012).

3   Paul Gronke, Eva Galanes-Rosenbaum, and Peter A. Miller, "Convenience Voting," *Annual Review of Political Science* 11 (2008): 437–455. It should be noted that convenience voting facilities for citizens differ from reforms modernizing electoral procedures, which are designed to make electoral administration easier for managers, such as the use of electronic machines rather than paper ballots.

4   Anthony Downs, *An Economic Theory of Voting* (New York: Harper, 1957).

5   http://www.ncsl.org/research/elections-and-campaigns/voter-id.aspx. For details, see Pippa Norris, *Strengthening Electoral Integrity* (New York: Cambridge University Press, 2017, forthcoming), chapter 9.

6   Lorraine Carol Minnite, *The Myth of Voter Fraud* (Ithaca: Cornell University Press, 2010); John S. Ahlquist, Kenneth R. Mayer, and Simon Jackman, "Alien Abduction and Voter Impersonation in the 2012 U.S. General Election: Evidence from a Survey List Experiment," *Election Law Journal* 13, no. 4 (2014): 460–475.

7 https://www.brennancenter.org/election-2016-controversies.

8 http://www.ncsl.org/research/elections-and-campaigns/
voter-id-history.aspx.

9 http://www.ncsl.org/research/elections-and-campaigns/
electronic-or-online-voter-registration.aspx; Electoral Assistance
Commission, *The 2014 EAC Election Administration and Voting
Survey Comprehensive Report* (2015), http://www.eac.gov/research/
election_administration_and_voting_survey.aspx.

10 See, for example, Louis Massicotte, Andre Blais, and Antoine
Yoshinaka, *Establishing the Rules of the Game* (Toronto: University
of Toronto Press, 2004).

11 Electoral Assistance Commission, *The 2014 EAC Election
Administration and Voting Survey Comprehensive Report* (2015),
http://www.eac.gov/research/election_administration_and_voting_
survey.aspx.

12 Barry C. Burden, David T. Canon, Kenneth R. Mayer, and
Donald P. Moynihan, "Election Laws, Mobilization, and Turnout:
The Unanticipated Consequences of Election Reform," *American
Journal of Political Science* 58, no. 1 (2014): 95–109.

13 Lonna Rae Atkeson, R. Michael Alvarez, and Thad E. Hall et al.,
"Balancing Fraud Prevention and Electoral Participation: Attitudes
toward Voter Identification," *Social Science Quarterly* 95, no. 5
(2014): 1381–1398.

14 Debate about the extent of electoral fraud is heated. Thus some
estimates find incidents of electoral fraud in recent US elections to be
trivial or nonexistent. See, for example, Minnite, *The Myth of Voter
Fraud*. Others counter that the threats are real. See, for example, Jesse T.
Richman, Gulshan A. Chattha, and David C. Earnest, "Do Non-citizens
Vote in US Elections?" *Electoral Studies* 36 (2014): 149–157.

15 Sari Horwitz, "How North Carolina Became the Epicenter of the
Voting Rights Battle," *Washington Post*, April 26, 2016, https://www.

washingtonpost.com/world/national-security/how-north-carolina-became-the-epicenter-of-the-voting-rights-battle/2016/04/26/af05c5a8-0bcb-11e6-8ab8-9ad050f76d7d_story.html.

16 http://www.nytimes.com/2016/08/22/us/politics/donald-trump-a-rigged-election-and-the-politics-of-race.html?_r=0.

17 http://www.ncsl.org/research/elections-and-campaigns/policies-for-election-observers.aspx.

18 Justin Levitt, *The Truth about Voter Fraud* (New York: Brennan Center for Justice 2007); https://www.brennancenter.org/issues/voter-fraud.

19 Sami Edge, "No Voter Fraud Isn't a Persistent Problem." *Washington Post*, September 1, 2012, https://www.washingtonpost.com/news/post-nation/wp/2016/09/01/voter-fraud-is-not-a-persistent-problem/?tid=a_inl&utm_term=.0ab16ed5cf7b.

20 Gallup Polls, August 15–16 2016. "About Six in 10 Confident in Accuracy of US Vote Count," http://www.gallup.com/poll/195371/six-confident-accuracy-vote-count.aspx?g_source=Politics&g_medium=newsfeed&g_campaign=tiles.

21 Emily Guskin and Scott Clement, "Poll: Nearly Half of Americans Say that Voter Fraud Occurs Often," *Washington Post*, September 15, 2016, https://www.washingtonpost.com/news/the-fix/wp/2016/09/15/poll-nearly-half-of-americans-say-voter-fraud-occurs-often.

22 Emily Beaulieu, "From Voter ID to Party ID: How Political Parties Affect Perceptions of Election Fraud in the US," *Electoral Studies* 35 (2014): 24–32.

23 http://www.nbcnews.com/politics/politics-news/nsa-chief-potential-russian-hacking-u-s-elections-concern-n647491.

24 Ben Wofford, "How to Hack an Election," *Politico*, August 5, 2016, http://www.politico.com/magazine/story/2016/08/2016-elections-russia-hack-how-to-hack-an-election-in-seven-minutes-214144.

25 Pippa Norris and Andrea Abe van Es, eds., *Checkbook Elections? Political Finance in Comparative Perspective* (New York: Oxford University Press, 2016).

26 Richard Hanson, *Plutocrats United: Campaign Money, the Supreme Court, and the Distortion of American Elections* (New Haven: Yale University Press, 2016).

27 The Center for Responsive Politics, https://www.opensecrets.org.

28 http://www.bbc.com/news/election-us-2016-35713168.

29 For details, see Norris and van Es, *Checkbook Elections?*; Hanson, *Plutocrats United.*

30 See Raymond J. La Raja and Brian F. Schaffner, *Campaign Finance and Political Polarization* (Ann Arbor: University of Michigan Press, 2015).

31 Norris and van Es, *Checkbook Elections?*; Robert G. Boatright, ed., *The Deregulatory Moment? A Comparative Perspective on Changing Campaign Finance Laws* (Michigan: University of Michigan Press, 2015); http://www.opensecrets.org/pres16.

32 http://www.nbcnews.com/politics/2016-election/updated-ad-spending-clinton-68-million-trump-4-million-n636486.

33 Thomas E. Patterson, "News Coverage of the 2016 Presidential Primaries: Horse Race Reporting Has Consequences," (Shorenstein Center, 2016). http://shorensteincenter.org/news-coverage-2016-presidential-primaries.

34 Robert F. Bauer and Benjamin L. Ginsberg et al., *The American Voting Experience: Report and Recommendations of the Presidential Commission on Election Administration* (Washington, DC, 2014). For more details, see www.supportthevoter.gov.

35 Bauer and Ginsberg et al., *The American Voting Experience.*

36 Pew Charitable Trust, *Election Performance Index* (2014), http://www.pewtrusts.org/en/multimedia/data-visualizations/2014/

elections-performance-index#intro. Data from 2008 to 2012 are currently available.

37 Pew Charitable Trust, "State Election Sites Crashed on Election Day," November 6, 2014, http://www.pewtrusts.org/en/about/news-room/news/2014/11/06/where-did-voters-look-to-find-their-polling-places.

38 *Hartford Courant*, "Anatomy of a Flawed Election," November 9, 2014, http://www.courant.com/community/hartford/hc-hartford-voting-problems-p-20141108-story.html#page=2.

39 *Chicago Sun Times*, "Calls to Election Judges a 'Serious Attempt to Disrupt' Voting," November 4, 2014, http://chicago.suntimes.com/chicago-politics/7/71/154384/calls-to-election-judges-a-serious-attempt-to-disrupt-voting.

40 *Washington Post*, "Voting Machine Problems in Newport News, Va. Beach," November 4, 2014, http://www.washingtonpost.com/local/virginians-deciding-senate-congressional-races/2014/11/4/33164a92-63f9-11e4-ab86-46e1d35_story.html.

41 *Bloomberg Politics*, "Your Guide to 2014 Midterm Election Voting Problems," November 4, 2014, http://www.bloomberg.com/politics/articles/2014-11-4/your-guide-to-2014-midterm-election-voting-problems.

42 *New York Times*, "As New Rules Take Effect, Voters Report Problems in Some States," November 4, 2014, http://www.nytimes.com/2014/11/5/us/election-tests-new-rules-on-voting.html.

43 R. Michael Alvarez and Thad E. Hall, "Controlling Democracy: The Principal Agent Problems in Election Administration," *Policy Studies Journal* 34, no. 4 (2006): 491–510; R. Michael Alvarez and Thad E. Hall, "Building Secure and Transparent Elections through Standard Operating Procedures," *Public Administration Review* 68, no. 5 (2008): 828–838; R. Michael Alvarez, Thad E. Hall, and Llewellyn Morgan, "Who Should Run Elections in the United States?" *Policy Studies Journal* 36, no. 3 (2008): 325–346; Hasen,

The Voting Wars; Burden and Stewart III, *The Measure of American Elections*.

44 See reports and data on these matters in US elections compiled by the Brennan Center for Justice. http://www.brennancenter.org/ and the National Conference of State Legislatures, http://www.ncsl. org/.

45 Alvarez, Hall, and Morgan, "Who Should Run Elections in the United States?"

46 Jonathan Salant, "Will the Federal Election Commission Ever Work Again?" *Bloomberg BusinessWeek*, May 2013. http://www. businessweek.com/articles/2013-05-02/will-the-federal-election-commission-ever-work-again.

47 http://www.eac.gov/about_the_eac/help_america_vote_act.aspx.

48 See, for example, the National Conference of State Legislatures http://www.ncsl.org.

II. Measuring Electoral Integrity

1 Pippa Norris, "The New Research Agenda Studying Electoral Integrity," Special issue of *Electoral Studies* 32, no. 4 (2013).

2 In addition, in 2014 elections in Haiti, Lebanon, and Comoros were delayed or suspended. Those are thus not included in the dataset. The election in Thailand was held and later annulled. There were also elections in North Korea and Trinidad and Tobago but with too few responses. These cases are excluded from the dataset.

3 Andreas Schedler, "The Menu of Manipulation," *Journal of Democracy* 13, no. 2 (2002): 36–50.

4 For more details, see Norris, *Strengthening Electoral Integrity*.

5 Pippa Norris, Ferran Martinez i Coma, and Richard Frank, "Assessing the Quality of Elections," *Journal of Democracy* 24,

no. 4 (2013): 124–135; Pippa Norris, Richard W. Frank, and Ferran Martinez i Coma, eds., *Advancing Electoral Integrity* (New York: Oxford University Press, 2014); Ferran Martínez i Coma and Carolien Van Ham, "Can Experts Judge Elections? Testing the Validity of Expert Judgments for Measuring Election Integrity" *European Journal of Political Research* (2015): doi:10.1111/1475-6765.12084; Pippa Norris, Richard W. Frank and Ferran Martínez i Coma, "Measuring Electoral Integrity around the World: A New Dataset," *PS: Political Science & Politics* 47, no. 4 (2014): 789–798.

6 Including the combined Freedom House/imputed Polity measure of democratization (R=.762** N. 151), and the Varieties of Democracy measure of electoral democracy (polyarchy) (R=.824**, N.140). Jan Teorell, Stefan Dahlberg, Sören Holmberg, Bo Rothstein, Felix Hartmann, and Richard Svensson, *The Quality of Government Standard Dataset*, version Jan.16 (University of Gothenburg: The Quality of Government Institute, 2016), http://www.qog.pol.gu.se.

III. Comparing Electoral Integrity within and across States

1 For more details, see Freedom House, *Freedom in the World* (2016), https://freedomhouse.org/report-types/freedom-world#. VcDNupNViko.

2 See Pippa Norris, Ferran Martínez i Coma, Alessandro Nai, and Max Grömping, *The Year in Elections, 2014. Sydney: The Electoral Integrity Project* (Sydney: University of Sydney, 2015).

3 Pippa Norris, *Why Electoral Integrity Matters* (New York: Cambridge University Press, 2014).

4 See also Sarah Birch, "Electoral Institutions and Popular Confidence in Electoral Processes: A Cross-national Analysis," *Electoral Studies* 27, no. 2 (2008): 305–320; Sarah Birch, "Perceptions

of Electoral Fairness and Voter Turnout," *Comparative Political Studies* 43, no. 12 (2010): 1601–1622.

5 See the Global Commission on Elections, Democracy and Security, *Deepening Democracy: A Strategy for Improving the Integrity of Elections Worldwide* (Sweden: IDEA, 2012); Joshua Tucker, "Enough! Electoral Fraud, Collective Action Problems, and Post-communist Colored Revolutions," *Perspectives on Politics* 5, no. 3 (2007): 535–551; Norris, Frank, and Martinez i Coma, "Contentious Elections: From Votes to Violence."

6 Factor analysis with principle component rotation was used to check the dimensionality of the ANES 2012 scale.

IV. What Is to Be Done?

1 Bauer and Ginsberg et al., *The American Voting Experience*. For more details, see www.supportthevoter.gov.

2 For more details, see Norris, *Strengthening Electoral Integrity*.

3 National Conference of State Legislative (NCSL) Election Law Database, 2014, http://www.ncsl.org/research/elections-and-campaigns/voter-id-history.aspx.

4 M. Qvortup, "First Past the Postman: Voting by Mail in Comparative Perspective," *Political Quarterly* 76, no. 3 (2005): 414–419; S. Luechinger, M. Rosinger, and A. Stutzer, "The Impact of Postal Voting on Participation: Evidence for Switzerland," *Swiss Political Science Review* 13 (2007): 167–122; Colin Rallings, Michael Thrasher, and G. Borisyuk, "Much Ado about Not Very Much: The Electoral Consequences of Postal Voting at the 2005 British General Election," *British Journal of Politics & International Relations* 12, no. 2 (2011): 223–238.

5 Kaat Smets and Carolien van Ham, "The Embarrassment of Riches? A Meta-analysis of Individual-level Research on Voter Turnout," *Electoral Studies* 32, no. 2 (2013): 344–359.

6   Steven J. Rosenstone and Raymond E. Wolfinger, "The Effect of Registration Laws on Voter Turnout," *American Political Science Review* 72 (1978): 27–45.

7   Francis Fox Piven and Richard A. Cloward, *Why Americans Don't Vote* (New York: Pantheon, 1988).

8   Burden, Canon, Mayer, and Moynihan, "Election Laws, Mobilization, and Turnout."

9   Adam J. Berinsky, "The Perverse Consequences of Electoral Reform in the United States," *American Politics Research* 33, no. 4 (2005): 471–491; Benjamin Highton, "Voter Registration and Turnout in the United States," *Perspectives on Politics* 2 (September, 2004): 57–15; Marjorie Randon Hershey, "What We Know about Voter-ID Laws, Registration, and Turnout," *PS-Political Science & Politics* 42, no. 1 (2009): 87–91.

10   Michael J. Hanmer, *Discount Voting: Voter Registration Reforms and Their Effects* (New York: Cambridge University Press, 2009); Shaun Bowler and Todd Donovan, "The Limited Effects of Election Reforms on Efficacy and Engagement," *Australian Journal of Political Science* 47, no. 1 (2011): 55–57; Pippa Norris., "Will New Technology Boost Turnout?," in *Electronic Voting and Democracy: A Comparative Analysis*, ed. Norbert Kersting and Harald Baldersheim (London: Palgrave, 2004), 193–225.

11   Burden, Canon, Mayer, and Moynihan, "Election Laws, Mobilization, and Turnout"; Berinsky, "The Perverse Consequences of Electoral Reform in the United States."

12   Burden, Canon, Mayer, and Moynihan, "Election Laws, Mobilization, and Turnout."

13   UK Electoral Commission, http://www.electoralcommission.org.uk/find-information-by-subject/electoral-fraud/electoral-fraud-vulnerabilities-review.

14   Atkeson, Alvarez, and Hall et al., "Balancing Fraud Prevention and Electoral Participation."

15 Alan Wall, Andrew Ellis, Ayman Ayoub, Carl W. Dundas, Joram Rukambe, and Sara Staino, *Electoral Management Design: The International IDEA Handbook* (Sweden: International IDEA, 2006).See also Joel Baxter, "Techniques for Effective Election Management," in *Elections: Perspectives on Establishing Democratic Practices* (New York: UN Department for Development Support and Management Services, 1997).

16 Alvarez, Hall, and Morgan, "Who Should Run Elections in the United States?"

17 Wall et al., *Electoral Management Design.*

18 Wall et al., *Electoral Management Design.*

19 Massicotte, Blais, and Yoshinaka, *Establishing the Rules of the Game.*

20 http://www.eac.gov/.

21 Wall et al., *Electoral Management Design.*

22 Christopher Pollitt and Gerrt Bouckaart, *Public Management Reform: A Comparative Analysis* (Oxford: Oxford University Press, 2004).

23 Pollitt and Bouckaart, *Public Management Reform.*

24 Chris Hanretty and Christel Koop, "Shall the Law Set Them Free? The Formal and Actual Independence of Regulatory Agencies," *Regulation & Governance* 7 (2013): 195–214.

25 Wall et al., *Electoral Management Design.*

26 Wall et al., *Electoral Management Design*, pp. 7–16.

27 Mark Thatcher, "Delegation to Independent Regulatory Agencies: Pressures, Functions and Contextual Mediation," *West European Politics* 25, no. 1 (2002): 125–147.

28 Wall et al., *Electoral Management Design.*

29 Bauer and Ginsberg et al., *The American Voting Experience.* For more details, see www.supportthevoter.gov.

30 See, for example, http://www.openelectiondata.net/en/guide/ electoral-integrity/public-confidence. "Public confidence in each step of an election process is critical to the integrity of the election. Citizens not only have a right to participate in elections, they have a right to know for themselves whether the electoral process is valid. Access to information about each phase of the election process is fundamental to creating and reinforcing public confidence in elections."

31 The Open Society Foundation, https://www.opensociety foundations.org/topics/freedom-information.

32 Wall et al., *Electoral Management Design*, p. 24.

33 Archon Fung, Mary Graham, and David Weil, eds., *Full Disclosure: The Perils and Promise of Transparency* (New York: Cambridge University Press, 2008).

34 Hasen, *The Voting Wars.*

35 Boatright, *The Deregulatory Moment?*

36 International IDEA, *The Handbook of Electoral Justice* (Stockholm: International IDEA, 2010).

V. Conclusions and Recommendations

1 David Easton, *A Systems Analysis of Political Life* (New York: Wiley, 1965).

2 Pippa Norris, ed., *Critical Citizens* (New York: Oxford University Press, 1999).

About the Author

Pippa Norris is the Paul McGuire Lecturer in Comparative Politics at Harvard University, Professor of Government and International Relations at the University of Sydney, and founding Director of the Electoral Integrity Project. Her recent books on electoral integrity for Cambridge University Press are *Why Electoral Integrity Matters* (2014), *Why Elections Fail* (2015), and *Strengthening Electoral Integrity* (2017).

CPSIA information can be obtained
at www.ICGtesting.com
Printed in the USA
LVOW06s1933060917
547768LV00007B/38/P

9 781501 713408